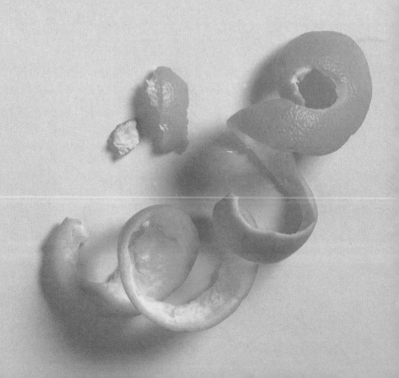

ORANGES

HARLAXTON
PUBLISHING

BRIDGET JONES

Harlaxton Publishing Limited
2 Avenue Road
Grantham
Lincolnshire NG31 6TA United Kingdom
A Member of the Weldon International Group of Companies.

First published in 1993.

© 1993	Copyright Harlaxton Publishing Limited
© 1993	Copyright design Harlaxton Publishing Limited
Publisher:	Robin Burgess
Design & Coordination:	Rachel Rush
Cover Photography:	Chris Allen, Forum Advertising Limited
Food Photography:	James Duncan
Stylist:	Madelaine Brehaut
Home Economist:	Joanna Farrow
Illustrator:	Valerie Littlewood
Editor:	Alison Leach
Typesetting:	John Macauley, Seller's, Grantham, UK
Colour separation:	GA Graphics, Stamford UK
Printing:	Imago, Singapore

British Library Cataloguing-in-Publication data.
A catalogue record for this book is available from the British Library.

Title:	Oranges
ISBN:	1-85837-105-8

 # CONTENTS

INTRODUCTION
4
DISCOVERING ORANGES
8
SALADS & STARTERS
15
MAIN DISHES
20
LIGHT MEALS
29
PRESERVES
37
DESSERTS
42
BAKING
50
SWEET NOTHINGS
58
INDEX
63

 **INTRODUCTION**

Considering their full flavour and juicy characteristics, it is hardly surprising that, together with apples, oranges are the most popular fruit for everyday consumption. This citrus fruit can also play a star role in great culinary productions.

Originating in China, oranges are now cultivated in warmer regions worldwide, from the South of France and other Mediterranean countries to the USA.

In 17th-century France the fashion for orangeries flourished among royalty and the aristocracy, the most famous being the one built at the Palace of Versailles. By this time oranges were so popular in Great Britain that they were sold by girls around the theatres of London, probably as a guise for other more personal wares on offer. Nell Gwyn secured a place in history for these girls, not so much for the sale of fruit as for her relationship with Charles II.

 **COOK'S NOTES**

Standard spoon and cup measurements are used in all recipes. All spoon and cup measurements are level.
1 tablespoon = 15 ml spoon
1 teaspoon   = 5 ml spoon
As the imperial/metric/US equivalents are not exact, follow only one system of measurement.
Ovens should be preheated to the specified temperature.
Fresh herbs are used unless otherwise stated. If they are unavailable, use half the quantity of dried herbs.
Use freshly ground black pepper unless white is indicated. Salt and pepper is added according to your individual taste.
Use only natural vanilla essence (extract) and not synthetic vanilla flavouring.

OPPOSITE: One-step Crystallized Peel (p.9) with Chocolate Orange Sticks (p.9)

  4

 **TYPES OF ORANGES**

Although many varieties are grown, the two key types are bitter oranges and sweet oranges. Probably the best known of the bitter group is the Seville orange but there are other varieties with the same characteristics of strong flavour and tart taste. Bitter oranges are used in cooking, and are the essential fruit for making famous British breakfast marmalade. Bitter or sour oranges are also used for making a classic bigarrade sauce, although modern versions combine lemon with oranges when the bitter variety is not available.

BITTER ORANGES have only a short season in the very early spring, so it is important to look out for them if you are planning to make a quantity of marmalade. Fortunately, they freeze extremely well, either prepared or whole. Their flavour is so pronounced that a strip of the rind added to a light commercial fruit or herb tea makes an aromatic drink. Their peel is ideal for making candied peel.

SWEET ORANGES are available throughout the year, with different varieties according to the season, and depending on market conditions world-wide. Jaffa, Valencia, Washington Navel or Navelina and Shamouti are among the best known of sweet oranges, appreciated for their size, sweetness and/or juiciness, but there is usually also a choice of less celebrated names, all of good quality. Navel oranges are seedless, which is worth remembering when buying fruit for cooking. With the growing popularity of domestic juicers, many supermarkets now stock large bags of oranges specifically chosen for their juice-yielding qualities.

BLOOD ORANGES are small, very juicy and sweet. They take their name from the blood-red flecks of colour in the flesh. Depending on the type of fruit, the skin may also be tinged with red or even be quite deep red.

The attractive orange colour of the peel is a phenomenon of fruit grown in cooler climates; fruit grown in tropical countries remains green. Apparently this is all due to the strength of the sun – it certainly has nothing to do with the ripeness of the fruit as you will know if you have ever visited a tropical country and eaten bright green oranges and lemons. Another interesting fact is that an orange tree bears both fruit and flowers simultaneously, making it an appealing subject for artists.

 **BUYING, STORING & PREPARING**

BUYING
When buying oranges, look for firm fruit with a fresh appearance. Avoid any oranges that feel soft and loose-skinned or with peel that looks limp and dull. Oranges keep well in a cool room for up to a week but they become mouldy if they are piled in a dish and left in a warm place. It is best to spread the oranges out in a shallow dish to avoid squashing the fruit underneath.

STORING
Oranges may be frozen whole if they are to be cut up for cooking at a later date; however, this is only necessary for the bitter variety which has such a short season. It is a good idea to keep a small container of grated rind in the freezer and to get into the habit of adding the rind from oranges before peeling them. Pared and shredded rind is also a useful freezer ingredient. Orange slices may be open-frozen, then packed and stored ready for adding to cold drinks or to tea (a slice of orange goes well in smoky teas, such as lapsang souchong).

PARING
You will find the term 'pared' used in the preparation of all citrus fruits. This means only the rind from the fruit is removed in one long strip (unless otherwise stated) without cutting off any of the white pith. The rind may be pared off around the fruit, in which case it will curl, or it may be cut off vertically in shorter strips. The former method is more suitable when a recipe calls for long shreds of pared rind. The shreds may be cooked, drained and used for garnish or decoration.

PEELING ORANGES
The easiest way to remove the peel is to make four cuts down the fruit from top to bottom at quarter-segment intervals. Then ease the peel off at the top point of each quarter and it will pull away cleanly.

If the orange is to be sliced or you wish to remove the segments, then the peel, pith and fine membrane around the fruit must first be cut away. To do this, cut off the peel and pith at the top and bottom of the orange. Stand the fruit on a board and use a sharp serrated knife to cut off strips of peel working down the orange and in strips around it. Trim off any small pieces of pith and you will be left with just the flesh of the fruit and inner membranes.

REMOVING SEGMENTS
When the fruit is free of all peel, pith and outer membrane, hold it over a basin, then use a sharp serrated knife to cut into the centre and ease out a segment by pushing the knife against the nearest membrane that divides the segments. Once you have removed one segment, the rest are easily cut out because you can see the membranes. Slice cleanly down the side of each segment as far in as the centre, then ease out each segment in turn. Squeeze any juice from the core and remaining membrane before discarding it.

DISCOVERING ORANGES

Whereas the recipes offer a range of specific ways in which to cook with oranges, the ideas on the following pages are intended to inspire you into discovering a broader use of the fruit

ORANGE GARNISHES & DECORATIONS

Oranges may be used in much the same way as lemons to garnish appropriate savoury dishes and decorate desserts or cakes. The large size of the fruit makes it ideal for cutting in half using the vandyke technique or for scooping out and then using as one or two containers.

- o   Use halved orange shells as novel containers for piped, hot creamy mashed potatoes with carrots.
- o   Present savoury or sweet salads in orange halves.
- o   Make a fresh fruit jelly with orange juice, the grated rind of the fruit, sugar, gelatine and water. Pour the liquid into the orange shells to set. Decorate with fruit segments and whipped cream.
- o   Pack ice-cream or sorbet into orange shells and re-freeze.

SPEEDY ORANGE CHOCOLATES

This is a good idea for children. Knead the grated rind of 1 orange into 125 g/4 oz sugarpaste or roll-out icing. Roll small pieces of the paste into balls. Use a fork to dip the balls into melted chocolate, allow the excess chocolate to drip off and place on wax paper. Top each one with a piece of candied orange peel and leave to set.

MARZIPAN ORANGES

Knead the grated rind of 1 orange and a little orange food colouring into 225 g/8 oz marzipan (almond paste). Roll small portions of the paste into balls about the size of grapes or small cherries. Then roll each ball of paste lightly on a nutmeg grater to give it the appearance of orange peel. Flatten the top of each marzipan 'orange' slightly. Remove the stalk and round bud from a clove and press the remaining small piece on the top of the 'orange'.

One-step Crystallized Peel

Making proper candied peel takes well over a week as the fruit rind has to be cooked and soaked in syrups of different densities until it is thoroughly impregnated with sugar. This is a quick alternative way of crystallizing rind which can be used in cooking or if coated with chocolate, is excellent served with after-dinner coffee.

Cut the rind off 4 large oranges lengthways in four segments. Cut each segment lengthways into four to six pieces and place in a saucepan. Cover with cold water and bring to the boil. Reduce the heat and simmer the rind for 20 minutes.

Drain and reserve 600 ml/1 pint/2$\frac{1}{2}$ cups of the liquid. Return the liquid to the pan and add 450 g/1 lb/2 cups granulated sugar. Stir until the sugar has dissolved, then add the rind and bring to the boil. Reduce the heat at once so that the syrup simmers, and cook for 1 hour. Pile some granulated sugar on a plate. Drain the rind thoroughly, reserving the syrup for use in desserts, and roll each piece thoroughly in the sugar. Spread out on wax paper or polythene and leave in a warm place until firm and dry. Store in an airtight container.

To make Chocolate Orange Sticks, cut pieces of the peel and dip them into melted chocolate until half or completely coated. Leave on wax paper to dry.

ABOVE: Gift boxes containing Marzipan Oranges and Speedy Orange Chocolates

 ## Orange Tea

For two cups, place 1 teaspoon China tea in a warmed pot. Add the pared rind of ½ orange, 1 cinnamon stick and 2 cloves. Pour in freshly boiling water and leave to brew for 15 minutes before pouring. Sweeten to taste and serve with a slice of orange.

Seville Refresher

This may not look terribly tempting as the orange is already squeezed but it tastes wonderful! Cut a quarter segment from a Seville or bitter orange and squeeze its juice through a coarse tea strainer into a tall glass. Discard any pips (seeds) from the fruit, then pop the segment into the glass too. Add a dash of bitters and a sprig of mint, and top up with sparkling mineral water.

Orange Vodka or Brandy

This is another drink to make when bitter oranges are available but sweet fruit may also be used. Pare the rind from a couple of oranges and coax it into a clean screw-topped bottle. Pour in vodka or brandy to fill the bottle and tap it to release any trapped air bubbles. Cover, label and store for at least a month before using.

To sweeten the spirit and make a liqueur, prepare a sugar syrup with 125 g/4 oz/ ½ cup granulated sugar and 125 ml/4 fl oz/ ½ cup water. Add the rind to the water and sugar, bring to the boil and stir until the sugar has dissolved. Pour into the bottle when cooled slightly, adding the rind. Top up with vodka or brandy, cover and label.

Orange Rum Cooler

Place a couple of ice cubes in a tall glass and add white rum to quarter-fill the glass. Add a couple of cucumber slices, a slice of orange, a mint sprig, and the juice of 1 large fresh orange. Top up with sparkling mineral or tonic water.

Buck's Fizz

Half-fill a glass with freshly squeezed orange juice and top it up with chilled sparkling dry white wine or champagne.

OPPOSITE: LEFT TO RIGHT: Orange Rum Cooler; Orange Vodka; Buck's Fizz

 **LASTING POT-POURRI**

Remember that you can add strips of orange rind to home-made pot-pourri. Small fir cones, dried seed or flower heads, such as cloves, cinnamon or cassia, sandalwood raspings, small bay leaves, rosemary, savory, thyme and lavender may all be used to extend a small amount of purchased pot-pourri or to revive an old mixture which has lost its scent. Place all the 'ingredients' in a polythene bag, adding some orris root powder if available, and sprinkle with 4 - 6 tablespoons of salt (for a medium-sized bag) to act as a preservative, particularly for the orange rind. Close the bag tightly and shake well, then leave in a dark place for a week, shaking the bag every day. Place the mixture in a bowl and stir it often to release its scent.

PEEL ROPE

Pare the rind from several oranges – you may like to make this over a couple of days as the fruit is eaten. Cut thinly around the fruit in fairly wide strips, taking care not to let them break, so that the rind curls naturally. Using a large darning needle and buttonhole thread, tie a knot in one end of the thread. Curl the rind around into a loose spiral, then push the needle and thread through the middle of the spiral. Thread as many spirals as you like, leaving a good length of spare thread unknotted.

Place in a polythene bag and sprinkle in a little ground cloves, a little ground cinnamon and 1 tablespoon orris root powder. Close the bag tightly and shake it well. Leave the bag in a dark place for a week.

To hang the room scenter, tie bows of ribbon between the spirals and at the ends of the thread. You may like to include a few small dried flowers secured with the ribbon. Remember to tie off the end of the thread when all the orange peel and bows are added.

ORANGE & HERB POT-POURRI

This is really a short-term room freshener which lasts well for a few days. It is a good way of using orange peel that would otherwise be discarded. Pare the rind from an orange, working around the fruit and cutting off fine, curly strips. Place the rind in a polythene bag. Wash and dry a handful of rosemary and thyme, then add them to the bag. Sprinkle in a few drops of eucalyptus oil and add 1 teaspoon sunflower oil. Close the bag tightly and shake well. Tip the mixture into a bowl and place it in a warm room. It will impart a scent if placed near a radiator.

OPPOSITE: CLOCKWISE: Lasting Pot-Pourri; Peel Rope; Orange & Herb Pot-Pourri; Exotic Bath Bouquet (p.14)

 **Exotic Bath Bouquet**

Mix the pared rind of 1 orange, cut into thin strips, with a handful of the spiky leaves from rosemary sprigs and a handful of lavender flowers in a polythene bag. Add a few drops of eucalyptus oil, close the bag and shake well. Use a third to a half of the mixture tied in a square of muslin (cheesecloth) and add this to the bath water. Keep the rest in a jar in the bathroom ready for the next time.

Orange Night-Light

This is a small version of a swede or turnip lantern.

Cut a shallow 'lid' from the top of a large orange. Squeeze out the juice, taking care not to damage the orange shell, and scoop out all the flesh. Cut a sliver from the bottom of the orange, if necessary, so that it stands level. Use a small sharp knife, or better still a craft knife or scalpel, to cut out a pattern in the side of the orange. Cut a hole in the centre of the orange 'lid'. Place a small night-light candle in the orange and light it, then put the 'lid' in position.

ABOVE: Orange Night-light

 # SALADS & STARTERS

If you have never thought beyond a Californian cocktail (grapefruit and orange) in terms of using oranges for the first course of a meal, then try some of these refreshing ideas.

Arabian Orange Salad

This slightly spicy salad is a most refreshing appetizer before a substantial main course; however, do remember that the flavours are quite strong, so do not follow it with a delicate main dish. Serve with plenty of warm pitta bread. The salad is also an excellent accompaniment for barbecues and grills, particularly pork, lamb or duck.

Serves 4

4	seedless oranges, peeled and sliced
12	black olives, stoned (pitted) and sliced
$\frac{1}{2}$	white or red onion, finely chopped
	A little grated nutmeg
45 g/1$\frac{1}{2}$ oz/$\frac{1}{3}$ cup	lightly salted shelled pistachio nuts, roughly chopped
	Olive oil

Arrange the orange slices in a shallow serving dish or in shallow individual bowls, overlapping them slightly. Sprinkle the olives and onion on top, then season with a little nutmeg before adding the pistachio nuts. Finally, trickle olive oil to taste over the salad. Cover and allow to stand for at least 2 hours before serving.

 **BAKED AVOCADOS**

SERVES 4	90 g/3 oz /1½ cups	fresh white breadcrumbs
	4	spring onions (scallions), finely chopped
	60 g/2 oz / ½ cup	walnuts, chopped
	1 tablespoon	chopped sage
	2 tablespoons	chopped parsley
		Grated rind of 1 orange
		Juice of ½ orange
		Salt and pepper
	2	large avocados
	4 tablespoons	melted butter
GARNISH		Sage sprigs
		Parsley sprigs

Mix the breadcrumbs with the spring onions, walnuts, sage, parsley and orange rind. Add seasoning to taste and mix in the orange juice to bind the ingredients. Halve the avocados and discard their stones (pits). Divide the breadcrumb mixture between them and stand them on a baking sheet, keeping the avocados upright by encircling them with crumpled foil.

Trickle the butter over the top of the stuffing and bake at 200°C/400°F/gas 6 for 20 minutes, until the top of the stuffing is lightly browned and the avocados are hot. Serve at once, garnished with sage and parsley sprigs.

 ## ORANGE-MARINATED MUSHROOMS

SERVES 4

6 tablespoons	olive oil
1	small onion, finely chopped
	Grated rind and juice of 1 orange
	Salt and pepper
2	garlic cloves, crushed
1 teaspoon	chopped marjoram
1 tablespoon	cider vinegar
450 g/1 lb	button mushrooms
2 tablespoons	chopped parsley
8	large basil leaves, shredded

GARNISH

Halved or quartered orange slices
Basil sprigs

Heat 2 tablespoons of the oil in a small saucepan and add the onion. Cook for 5 minutes, stirring. Whisk the orange rind and juice with seasoning, the garlic, marjoram and vinegar. Add the remaining oil to the cooked onion, remove from the heat and whisk in the orange mixture to make a slightly thickened dressing.

Place the mushrooms in a shallow bowl and pour the dressing over them. Mix well, cover and leave to marinate for at least 3 hours before serving, stirring occasionally.

Add the parsley and basil to the mushrooms just before serving. Mix well and transfer to individual dishes. Garnish with orange slices and basil sprigs. Serve with plenty of crusty bread to mop up the dressing.

OPPOSITE: CLOCKWISE: Baked Avocados; Orange-Marinated Mushrooms; Arabian Orange Salad (p.15)

 **Salad Ideas**

Here are just a few ways in which an orange can
transform simple ingredients into an exotic salad.

Mustard Orange Dressing

Mix together 1 tablespoon mild wholegrain mustard, $\frac{1}{2}$ teaspoon caster (superfine) sugar and plenty of seasoning.
Whisk in the juice of 1 orange and 1 tablespoon red wine vinegar. When the sugar has dissolved, gradually whisk in
125 ml/4 fl oz/ $\frac{1}{2}$ cup olive oil and a finely chopped garlic clove, if liked.

Refreshing Red Cabbage

Finely shred 225 g/8 oz/2$\frac{1}{2}$ cups red cabbage. Halve and very finely slice a mild onion, then separate the rings and add
them to the cabbage. Add 1 tablespoon chopped capers and seasoning to taste. Pare the rind from $\frac{1}{2}$ orange and shred
it finely, then cook it in boiling water for 10 minutes. Drain the rind and toss it into the salad. Whisk 125 ml/4 fl oz/ $\frac{1}{2}$
cup olive oil into the juice of 1 orange and pour this over the salad. Lastly, add the segments from 3 oranges and mix
them in lightly.

Tomato & Orange Salad

Arrange skinned and sliced tomatoes in a shallow dish with fresh orange segments. Sprinkle with snipped chives and
seasoning, then dress with a little light oil and vinegar dressing.

Zesty Carrot Salad

This is one of my favourite salads and it is a perfect summertime starter. Serve it with crusty bread or offer it as part of
a mixed hors d'oeuvre platter. The carrots must be really fresh and they should be coarsely grated – you need about
225 g/8 oz/2 cups for 4 - 6 servings. Sprinkle them with just a hint of salt and plenty of black pepper before adding the
grated rind of $\frac{1}{2}$ orange and the juice of a whole orange. If you are counting the calories, then leave it at that; if not trickle
good-quality olive oil to taste over the salad and toss it in. Cover and allow to stand for 1 hour before serving.

 **PIQUANT RAREBIT**

SERVES 4

As a change from the usual Welsh rarebit, try this interesting orange version.

Finely grate 225 g/8 oz/2 cups mature Cheddar cheese and place it in a small saucepan. Add 1 teaspoon dry English mustard, salt and pepper, the grated rind of $\frac{1}{2}$ orange and the juice of 1 orange.

Heat gently, stirring all the time, until the cheese melts and combines with the other ingredients. Remove from the heat and stir in 1 tablespoon snipped chives, then transfer to a small basin and leave to cool.

Toast 4 thick bread slices on one side, then toast the second sides very lightly. Spread with the rarebit mixture and grill (broil) until golden brown and bubbling. Serve at once.

ABOVE: TOP: Piquant Rarebit - BELOW: Zesty Carrot Salad

 # MAIN DISHES

Make a break from tradition with these alternative main dishes; for example, sample orange with mussels or a whole spiced chicken coated with a rich orange glaze. There are recipes for dinner parties, a roast for Sunday lunch or a quick stir-fry to share with friends.

MUSSELS WITH GARLIC-ORANGE SAUCE

SERVES 4

900 g/2 lb	mussels, scrubbed
2 tablespoons	olive oil
2	garlic cloves, crushed
$\frac{1}{2}$	onion, finely chopped
1	bay leaf
	Grated rind of 1 orange
	Juice of 2 oranges
	Salt and pepper

Pull off the dark, hairy beard which protrudes from the mussels and discard any opened shells which do not shut when tapped. Rinse well. Heat the oil in a large saucepan, add the garlic, onion and bay leaf, and cook for 5 minutes. Stir in the orange rind. Make up the orange juice to 250 ml/8 fl oz/1 cup with water if necessary and add it to the pan. Sprinkle in seasoning and simmer gently for 5 minutes.

Add the mussels, bring to the boil and reduce the heat slightly; then cover the pan tightly and cook for 5 - 6 minutes, until the mussels have opened. Strain, return the cooking juices to the pan and boil them hard until reduced by half. Divide the mussels discarding any which have not opened, between four dishes. Pour the reduced juices over the mussels and serve at once, with plenty of French bread to mop the sauce.

 ## Tuna with Orange

SERVES 4

$\frac{1}{2}$	small onion, chopped
1	bay leaf
8	coriander seeds, crushed
1	garlic clove, chopped
	Grated rind and juice of 1 orange
125 ml/4 fl oz/$\frac{1}{2}$ cup	red wine
125 ml/4 fl oz/$\frac{1}{2}$ cup	water
4 tablespoons	olive oil
	Salt and pepper
About 675 g/1$\frac{1}{2}$ lb	tuna steak, cut into 4 pieces
30 g/1 oz/2 tablespoons	butter
1 tablespoon	chopped parsley

Mix together the onion, bay leaf, coriander, garlic, orange rind and juice, wine, water, olive oil and seasoning in a small saucepan. Bring to the boil, reduce the heat and cover the pan. Simmer for 20 minutes, then allow to cool.

Arrange the pieces of tuna steak in a shallow dish and pour the cooled marinade over them. Cover and leave to marinate in the refrigerator overnight.

Drain the tuna and grill (broil) it for about 5 minutes on each side, depending on the thickness of the steak, brushing with the marinade occasionally. While the tuna is cooking, boil the marinade until it is reduced by half. Transfer the tuna to warmed plates and spoon some of the hot marinade over each portion. Serve at once.

NEXT PAGE: CLOCKWISE: Refreshing Red Cabbage (p.18); Turkey Olives (p.24); Duck Bigarrade (p.25)

 ## TURKEY OLIVES

SERVES 4	60 g/2 oz/ ^{1}⁄$_4$ cup	*butter*
	1	*small leek, chopped*
	90 g/3 oz/1^1⁄$_2$ cups	*fresh breadcrumbs*
	60 g/2 oz/ ^{1}⁄$_2$ cup	*walnuts, chopped*
	125 g/4 oz/^{2}⁄$_3$ cup	*cooked ham, chopped*
		Salt and pepper
	1 - 2 tablespoons	*milk*
	4	*turkey escalopes (about 575 g/1^1⁄$_4$ lb), beaten thin*
	300 ml/ ^{1}⁄$_2$ pint/1^1⁄$_4$ cups	*red wine*
	150 ml/ ^{1}⁄$_4$ pint/^{2}⁄$_3$ cup	*water*
		Grated rind and juice of 1 orange
	4 tablespoons	*redcurrant jelly*
	1 tablespoon	*arrowroot*
GARNISH		*Orange slices*
		Walnut halves

Melt half the butter in a small saucepan and add the leek. Cook for 5 minutes, remove from the heat, then stir in the breadcrumbs, walnuts, ham, seasoning and enough milk to bind the stuffing. Lay out the turkey escalopes and divide the stuffing between them. Fold the ends of the meat over, then fold the sides over and roll up to make a neat package. Tie securely with cooking string.

Melt the remaining butter in a flameproof casserole and brown the turkey escalopes. Add the wine, water, orange rind and juice and bring to simmering point. Cover tightly and cook for 45 minutes, turning the turkey olives halfway through cooking.

Transfer the turkey olives to a warmed serving dish, remove the string, cover and keep hot. Stir the redcurrant jelly into the sauce and heat until it has melted. Mix the arrowroot with a little water, then add to the sauce and bring to the boil. Remove from the heat at once and taste for seasoning.

Serve the turkey olives sliced and fanned out slightly, with the sauce poured over. Garnish with orange slices and walnut halves.

 **DUCK BIGARRADE**

SERVES 4

	Pared rind and juice of 1 bitter orange
1	*bay leaf*
2	*thyme sprigs*
2	*large boneless duck breasts, skinned and sliced into 12 mm/ ^{1}⁄2 inch thick medallions*
1 tablespoon	*oil*
2	*rindless bacon rashers (slices), cut into slivers*
1	*onion, halved and chopped*
2 tablespoons	*plain (all-purpose) flour*
300 ml/ ^{1}⁄2 pint/1^{1}4 cups	*duck or beef stock*
2 tablespoons	*soft brown sugar*

Cut the orange rind into fine shreds and cook it in boiling water for 5 minutes, then drain well. Mix the cooked rind and juice, bay and thyme with the duck in a bowl. Cover and marinate for at least 2 hours.

Heat the oil in a frying pan (skillet). Add the bacon, onion and drained duck (reserving the marinade) with the herbs and shredded rind. Cook, stirring, until the duck is lightly browned. Stir in the flour, then add the marinade and the stock. Bring to the boil, stirring, reduce the heat at once and add the sugar. Simmer very gently for 20 minutes, until the duck is cooked and the sauce well flavoured. Serve at once.

ORANGE-GLAZED LAMB

SERVES 4

Squeeze the juice from 3 large oranges and stir in 1 teaspoon sugar. Season 4 lamb steaks (slices off the leg) well and dust them lightly with plain (all-purpose) flour. Heat a little oil and butter together in a large frying pan (skillet). Add the steaks and cook until well browned, then turn them and cook the second side until browned. When the steaks are cooked to your liking, transfer them to a warmed serving platter and keep hot.

Add the orange juice to the pan and bring it to the boil, stirring all the cooking sediment off the pan. Boil rapidly until the juice is reduced by half or slightly more to form a full-flavoured glaze. Taste for seasoning, pour the glaze over the lamb steaks and serve at once.

 ## SKEWERED PORK

A bed of mixed wild and Basmati rice, tossed with
butter and chopped parsley, and a fresh green salad
are perfect accompaniments for these kebabs,
which are ideal barbecue candidates.

SERVES 4

675 g/1½ lb	lean boneless pork, cut in large cubes
2 tablespoons	Dijon mustard
	Grated rind and juice of 1 orange
2 tablespoons	brandy
1 tablespoon	chopped rosemary
	Salt and pepper
2	red (sweet bell) peppers, seeded and cut into chunks
2	onions, cut into large chunks

Place the pork in a bowl. Add the mustard, orange rind and juice, brandy, rosemary and seasoning. Mix the pork so that all the pieces are thoroughly coated with the flavouring ingredients. Cover and leave to marinate in the refrigerator overnight.

Thread the pork on to eight metal skewers, adding the pieces of red pepper and onion. Grill (broil) the kebabs, without placing them too near the heat, for 10-15 minutes on each side, or until the pork is thoroughly cooked. Baste with the remaining marinade during cooking to prevent the ingredients from drying out. Serve at once.

OPPOSITE: TOP: Sizzling Steak (p.28) - BOTTOM: Skewered Pork

 **SIZZLING STEAK**

This is a rich dish which tastes good with plain
cooked noodles.

SERVES 4

	Pared rind of ¹⁄₂ orange
	Juice of 1 orange
675 g/1¹⁄₂ lb	*frying steak, cut into fine strips*
1 teaspoon	*dried oregano*
2 tablespoons	*plain (all-purpose) flour*
	Salt and pepper
30 g/1 oz/2 tablespoons	*beef dripping*
1	*large onion, halved and thinly sliced*
1	*carrot, cut into short, fine strips (julienne)*
2	*celery sticks, cut into short, fine strips*
125 ml/4 fl oz / ¹⁄₂ cup	*water*
125 ml/4 fl oz / ¹⁄₂ cup	*port*
300 ml/ ¹⁄₂ pint/1¹⁄₄ cups	*soured (fresh sour) cream*
2 tablespoons	*chopped parsley*

Cut the orange rind into fine strips, cook them in boiling water for 15 minutes and drain well. Mix together the orange
rind, steak, oregano, flour and plenty of seasoning.

Melt the dripping in a large frying pan (skillet). Add the steak mixture and stir-fry the strips over a high heat until
lightly browned before adding the onion, carrot and celery. Continue cooking, stirring the mixture all the time, until the
steak is cooked and the vegetables are part-cooked.

Pour in the orange juice, water and port and bring to the boil. Reduce the heat slightly but keep the mixture bubbling
quite fast, stirring it frequently, until most of the liquid has evaporated and the vegetables are tender but still have
plenty of bite. Remove the pan from the heat, taste the mixture for seasoning and swirl in the soured cream, then
sprinkle in the parsley and serve at once.

 **LIGHT MEALS**

Wake up your taste-buds with these interesting dishes for light meals, from a rich Emmenthal Tart to marry with a crisp cold white wine to the simplest dish of tender barley tossed with delicious orange-seasoned pesto.

EMMENTHAL TART

Serves 6 - 8

125 g/4 oz/ ^{1}⁄2 cup	butter
175 g/6 oz/ 1^1⁄2 cups	plain (all-purpose) flour
About 2 tablespoons	water
	Salt and pepper
4	medium-thick bread slices, lightly toasted and crumbed
4 tablespoons	snipped chives
1 tablespoon	chopped sage
2 tablespoons	chopped parsley
1 teaspoon	chopped tarragon
	Grated rind of 1 orange
450 g/1 lb	ripe tomatoes, skinned and thinly sliced
450 g/1 lb	Emmenthal cheese, very thinly sliced

Rub the butter into the flour until the mixture resembles breadcrumbs and add just enough water to bind the mixture in clumps. Gather the dough together, roll it out and use it to line a 23 cm/9 inch round, loose-bottomed flan tin (pie pan). Prick the bottom of the pastry and chill the case for at least 30 minutes, then line it with greaseproof paper and baking beans and bake for 15 minutes at 200°C/400°F/gas 6. Remove the paper and beans. Cook for a further 5 minutes. Reduce the oven temperature to 180°C/350°F/gas 5.

Meanwhile, mix the toast crumbs, herbs, orange rind and seasoning. Sprinkle a thin layer of the crumbs in the base of the flan and top with cheese. Continue layering the crumbs and cheese until all the ingredients are used. Finish with a layer of cheese. Bake for about 30 minutes, until golden brown and bubbling hot. Serve at once.

 29

 **VEAL & HAM LOAF**

This is a meat loaf with a difference: an aromatic orange and ham stuffing is layered through the middle and it tastes terrific either hot or cold. Minced (ground) venison, lamb or beef may be substituted for the veal if you like.

SERVES 4 - 6

1	large onion, chopped
450 g/1 lb/2^{1}2 cups	minced (ground) veal
1 teaspoon	ground mace
	Salt and pepper
125 g/4 oz /2 cups	fresh white breadcrumbs
1	egg
1 tablespoon	oil
1	leek, roughly chopped
450 g/1 lb/2^{1}2 cups	cooked ham, cut into dice
	Grated rind and juice of 1 orange
4	large basil sprigs, shredded

Base-line and grease a 450 g/1 lb loaf tin (pan). Mix together the onion, veal, mace, seasoning, half the breadcrumbs and the egg. Pound the ingredients to make sure they are thoroughly combined and press half the mixture into the prepared tin.

Heat the oil in a small saucepan, add the leek and cook for about 5 minutes, stirring, until the leek has softened and reduced in volume. Remove from the heat and mix in the ham, remaining breadcrumbs, seasoning, orange rind and juice, and basil. Press this mixture into the tin over the veal and top with the remaining veal.

Cover the top of the meat loaf with greased greaseproof (wax) paper. Bake at 180°C/350°F/gas 4 for 1 hour, until the meat loaf is firm and cooked through. Leave to stand for 10 minutes before turning out and slicing. A sharp serrated knife is best for cutting neat slices.

 **FETTUCINI WITH BACON & FENNEL**

SERVES 4

3 tablespoons	olive oil
2	garlic cloves, crushed
	Pared rind of $\frac{1}{2}$ orange, cut into fine shreds
225 g/8 oz	rindless rashers (slices) bacon, cut into dice
2	fennel bulbs, halved and thinly sliced
1	large onion, halved and thinly sliced
450 g/1 lb	fettucini or tagliatelle
	Salt and pepper
2 tablespoons	tomato paste
400 g/14 oz	can chopped tomatoes
	Freshly grated Parmesan cheese, to serve

Heat the oil in a saucepan. Add the garlic, orange rind and bacon, and cook, stirring, for 2-3 minutes, until the bacon is firm. Then stir in the fennel and onion. Cover the pan and leave the vegetables to cook gently for 20 minutes.

Meanwhile, if using dried pasta cook in plenty of boiling salted water for about 12 minutes; fresh pasta cooks in 2-3 minutes so it can be prepared after the tomatoes are added to the sauce. Stir the tomato paste, tomatoes and seasoning into the fennel mixture. Bring to the boil, reduce the heat, cover the pan and simmer for a further 15 minutes.

Drain the pasta and place it in a serving dish. Pour the fennel mixture over and toss well. Serve at once with Parmesan cheese.

NEXT PAGE: CLOCKWISE: Mussels with Garlic-Orange Sauce (p.20); Veal and Ham Loaf; Fettucini with Bacon and Fennel

 ## One-Pot Sauté

Serves 4	
2 tablespoons	flaked almonds
30 g/1 oz/2 tablespoons	butter
2 tablespoons	olive oil
1	bay leaf
1	onion, chopped
1	celery stick, thinly sliced
450 g/1 lb	courgettes (zucchini), sliced
2 x 400 g/14 oz	cans chick-peas (garbanzo beans), drained
2 teaspoons	cornflour (cornstarch)
	Juice of 3 oranges
125 ml/4 fl oz/$\frac{1}{2}$ cup	dry white wine
2 tablespoons	chopped dill

Dry-fry the almonds in a large frying pan (skillet) or flameproof casserole. Stir the nuts continuously until they are browned, then remove them from the pan and set aside. Add the butter, oil and bay leaf. Sauté the onion and celery for 10 minutes before adding the courgettes and chick-peas. Sprinkle in seasoning and sauté the vegetables for 3 minutes, until the courgettes are half-cooked.

Mix the cornflour with some of the orange juice to make a smooth paste. Add the wine and remaining orange juice to the vegetable mixture and bring to the boil. Cook over medium heat, stirring often, for 3 minutes, until the courgettes are just tender. Stir in the cornflour and bring to the boil, stirring. Simmer for 2 minutes.

Serve the sautéed vegetables promptly, sprinkled with the dill and almonds, with crusty Granary bread or French bread to mop the juices.

New Potato Salad with Salami

SERVES 6

This is a tasty, piquant salad for summer lunch.
Serve it with thinly sliced bread and butter.

Cook 675 g/1½ lb new potatoes in boiling salted water until tender. Meanwhile, mix the grated rind and juice of 1 orange with 1 finely chopped garlic clove and 6-10 pitted black (ripe) olives. Immediately the potatoes are drained, pour the orange mixture over them, mix well and leave to cool.

Cut 225 g/8 oz salami into thin strips and chop 6 spring onions (scallions), then mix both into the potato salad. Add 250 ml/ 8 fl oz/1 cup mayonnaise and stir it into the salad until it is thoroughly combined with the orange juice in a thinned dressing. Serve the potato salad on a bed of shredded Iceberg lettuce or other crisp leaves and sprinkle with plenty of chopped parsley.

ABOVE: TOP: New Potato Salad with Salami - BOTTOM: One-Pot Sauté

 **BARLEY WITH ORANGE PESTO**

SERVES 4

Pesto is an Italian paste of garlic, basil, pine kernels, Parmesan cheese and olive oil. Tangy orange tastes excellent with the paste, especially when served with barley.

Purée a large handful of fresh basil, 2 garlic cloves, 60 g/2 oz/ ¹₂ cup freshly grated Parmesan cheese, the coarsely grated rind of 1 orange and 60 g/2 oz/ ¹₂ cup pine kernels in a blender, gradually adding 125 ml/4 fl oz/ ¹₂ cup olive oil. Stir in salt and pepper.

Place 225 g/8 oz/1¹₄ cups pearl barley in a saucepan. Add a little salt and 900 ml/1¹₂ pints/3³₄ cups water. Bring to the boil, reduce the heat and cover the pan tightly. Simmer gently for about 30 minutes, until most of the water has been absorbed and the barley is tender but still has a bit of bite. Drain any remaining water and serve the barley topped with the orange pesto, mixing well before eating. Make a simple green salad with fresh orange segments in it to complement the barley.

ABOVE: Barley with Orange Pesto

 # PRESERVES

Capture the unique essence of orange with this selection of varied, no-fuss recipes for savoury and sweet preserves which will readily transform any meal or snack into a sunshine-filled treat.

BEETROOT & ORANGE CHUTNEY

Cut chunky and made into either a quick-cook pickle or a finer chutney, as here, this is one of my favourite savoury preserves.

MAKES about 1.8 kg/4 lb

	Pared rind and juice of 1 large orange
450 g/1 lb	cooking apples, peeled, cored and sliced
450 g/1 lb	onions, chopped
125 g/4 oz/^{3}⁄4 cup	raisins
900 g/2 lb	uncooked beetroot, peeled and roughly chopped,
or 1.5 kg/3 lb	cooked vacuum-packed beetroot
1 tablespoon	ground coriander
1 tablespoon	ground ginger
2	garlic cloves, crushed
350 g/12 oz/2 cups	soft brown sugar
450 ml/^{3}⁄4 pint/2 cups	cider vinegar

Chop the pared orange rind. Place all the ingredients in a large saucepan. Bring to the boil, stirring continuously until the sugar has dissolved. Then reduce the heat so that the mixture simmers, cover the pan tightly and leave to cook for 1^1⁄2 hours. Stir the chutney occasionally during cooking to prevent it sticking to the pan.

Pot the chutney in sterilized, warmed jars. Cover immediately with wax paper and airtight, vinegar-proof lids. Label and allow to mature for at least a week before using.

 **ZESTY TOMATO CHUTNEY**

MAKES about 2.5 kg/5 lb

1	orange
450 g/1 lb	cooking apples, peeled, cored and chopped
900 g/2 lb	ripe tomatoes, skinned and chopped
900 g/2 lb	onions, chopped
200 g/7 oz/1$\frac{1}{2}$ cups	sultanas (golden raisins)
350 g/12 oz/2 cups	soft brown sugar
1 tablespoon	ground allspice
1 teaspoon	turmeric
600 ml/1 pint/2$\frac{1}{2}$ cups	malt vinegar

Discard the pips (seeds) from the orange as you chop it. Place the fruit in a large saucepan with all the other ingredients. Bring to the boil, stirring continuously, then reduce the heat and cover the pan. Simmer the chutney for 2 hours, stirring it occasionally. Then uncover the pan and cook for a further 1 hour.

Pot the chutney in sterilized, warmed jars. Cover immediately with wax paper and airtight, vinegar-proof lids. Label and allow to mature for at least a week before using.

ABOVE: LEFT TO RIGHT: Beetroot and Orange Chutney (p.37); Zesty Tomato Chutney

 RICH ORANGE & PEACH PRESERVE

This is an easy, throw-it-all-in preserve which is
enriched with cinnamon and brandy.

MAKES about 2.75 kg/6 lb	
450 g/1 lb	bitter oranges, chopped and pips (seeds) removed
450 g/1 lb	no-need-to-soak dried peaches, chopped
1	lemon, chopped and pips (seeds) removed
1	cinnamon stick
2.25 litres/4 pints/2½ quarts	water
150 g/5 oz/1 cup	raisins
1.8 kg/4 lb	granulated or preserving sugar
30 g/1 oz/2 tablespoons	unsalted butter
60 g/2 oz/½ cup	flaked almonds
125 ml/4 fl oz/½ cup	brandy

Place the oranges, peaches, lemon, cinnamon stick and water in a large saucepan. Bring to the boil, then reduce the
heat and cover the pan. Simmer the fruit steadily for 1 hour. Add the raisins and continue cooking for about 1 hour,
until the oranges are thoroughly cooked.

Remove the cinnamon stick and add the sugar. Make sure that there is plenty of room in the pan for the preserve to
boil – transfer it to a larger container if necessary. Stir until the sugar has dissolved completely, then bring the preserve
to a full rolling boil. Boil the preserve until setting point is reached: 104°C/220°F on a sugar thermometer or when a
little preserve placed on a cold saucer sets to form a distinct skin which will wrinkle when pushed with a fingertip.

Stir in the butter, almonds and brandy, and pot the preserve immediately in sterilized, warmed jars. Cover at once
with waxed discs and airtight lids. Store the preserve in a cool, dark place where it will keep for at least 6 months.

 ## Orange Redcurrant Jelly

Try this variation on tradition, the orange rind and spices give the jelly a pleasing fullness that makes it ideal for savoury and sweet uses. The quantity of jelly will depend on the yield of juice from the fruit.

	Pared rind and juice of 2 oranges
1	cinnamon stick
4	cloves
1	lemon, chopped and pips (seeds) discarded
900 g/2 lb	redcurrants
600 ml/1 pint/2^{1}₂ cups	water
	Granulated or preserving sugar

Place the orange rind and juice in a large saucepan with the cinnamon, cloves, lemon and redcurrants. Add the water and bring to the boil. Reduce the heat, cover the pan tightly and simmer the fruit for 1^{1}₂ hours, stirring occasionally. Leave to cool, then strain the fruit through a jelly bag overnight. Do not squeeze the bag or the jelly will be cloudy.

Measure the juice and return it to the clean pan. Add 450 g/1 lb/2 cups sugar for every 600 ml/1 pint/2^{1}₂ cups juice. Stir until the sugar has dissolved completely, then bring to a full rolling boil and boil until setting point is reached: 104°C/220°F on a sugar thermometer or when a little of the jelly placed on a cold saucer sets to form a skin which wrinkles when pushed with a fingertip.

 **SPECIAL PICKLED ONIONS**

MAKES about 1.5 kg/3 lb

Peel 1.5 kg/3 lb pickling onions and layer them in a bowl, sprinkling each layer generously with salt. Cover and leave to stand overnight, then drain, rinse briefly and dry well on paper towels. Pack the onions into sterilized jars, adding a slice of orange to each jar.

Pare the rind from a large orange and place it in a saucepan with 1 tablespoon coriander seeds, 2 slices fresh root ginger, 1 dried red chilli, 1 cinnamon stick, 1 teaspoon black peppercorns, 1 bay leaf, 5 cloves and 1 tablespoon mustard seeds. Bring to the boil, then reduce the heat, cover and simmer very gently for 30 minutes. Remove from the heat and leave until cold, then strain through fine muslin (cheesecloth).

Pour the spiced vinegar into the jars to cover the onions completely. Tap the jars to release any trapped air bubbles and add more vinegar if necessary. Cover with vinegar-proof lids, label and store for at least 2 weeks (if you can) before using.

ABOVE: Special Pickled Onions

 # DESERTS

This is one of the culinary areas where citrus fruit has an established role, so the following recipes need little introduction; however, there are a few original ideas to inspire the adventurous cook beyond traditional dishes.

RICH ORANGE ICE-CREAM

This is easy and particularly good. The suggested number of servings allows for scooping the ice-cream out of a container.

SERVES 6 - 8

600 ml/1 pint/2¹2 cups	double (heavy) cream
	Grated rind of 3 oranges
	Juice of 1 orange
1 tablespoon	natural vanilla essence (extract)
125 g/4 oz/³4 cup	icing (confectioners') sugar
125 g/4 oz/4 squares	plain (dark) chocolate
1 teaspoon	sweet almond oil
	Orange segments to serve

Place the cream in a large bowl and add the rind of 2 oranges, the juice, and vanilla. Stir in the icing sugar and whip the mixture until it stands in soft peaks. Turn the mixture into a freezer container and freeze overnight.

Melt the chocolate with the remaining orange rind in a bowl over a saucepan of hot water, stir in the almond oil and set aside to cool slightly. When ready to serve the dessert, spoon the chocolate into a small paper piping bag. Scoop the ice-cream into individual glass dishes. Snip just the tip off the piping bag and drizzle (or spin) the chocolate from side to side over the ice-cream. Decorate with orange segments and serve.

 ## CARAMELIZED PROFITEROLES

SERVES 4 - 6

60 g/2 oz/ ^{1}⁄4 cup	butter
125 ml/4 fl oz/ ^{1}⁄2 cup	water
75 g/2 ^{1}⁄2 oz/ ^{1}⁄3 cup	plain (all-purpose) flour
2	eggs
	Grated rind and juice of 2 oranges
225 g/8 oz/1 cup	granulated sugar
2 tablespoons	icing (confectioners') sugar
300 ml/ ^{1}⁄2 pint/1 ^{1}⁄4 cups	double (heavy) cream, whipped

Grease two baking sheets. Place the butter and water in a saucepan. Heat gently until the butter has melted, then bring to the boil quickly. Tip in all the flour as soon as the liquid is boiling rapidly, stir and remove the pan from the heat immediately. Stir the mixture until it forms a ball of paste but do not beat it. Allow to cool for 10 minutes, then beat in the eggs and beat hard until the paste is very smooth and glossy. Spoon the paste into a piping bag fitted with a large plain icing tube (tip) and pipe 20 portions of mixture well apart on the baking sheets.

Bake at 220°C/425°F/gas 7 for 10 minutes, then reduce the oven temperature to 190°C/375°F/gas 5 and cook for a further 10 minutes, or until the profiteroles are well puffed, golden and crisp. Slit them open immediately and cool on a wire rack.

Heat the orange juice and sugar, stirring until the sugar has dissolved. Bring to the boil, stop stirring and cook until the syrup turns a rich golden colour. Remove the pan from the heat, add half the orange rind and 2 tablespoons boiling water, taking great care as the caramel will spit. Set aside to cool completely.

Whip the remaining orange rind and the icing sugar into the cream until it stands in firm peaks. Fill the profiteroles with the whipped cream and pile them in a serving dish. Pour the caramel sauce over before serving.

NEXT PAGE: CLOCKWISE: Caramelized Orange Profiteroles; Rich Orange Ice-Cream; Strawberries with Orange Meringues (p.46)

 **STRAWBERRIES & MERINGUES**

This is the ultimate in serve-yourself desserts!

Serves 6	
4	*egg whites*
225 g/8 oz/1 cup	*caster (superfine) sugar*
	Grated rind of 1 orange
675 g/1½ lb	*strawberries, hulled*
6 tablespoons	*orange liqueur*
300 ml/½ pint/1¼ cups	*whipping cream, whipped*

Line two baking sheets with non-stick bakers' parchment. Whisk the egg whites until they are stiff and dry. Gradually whisk in the sugar and continue whisking until the meringue mixture is stiff and glossy. Fold in the orange rind and spoon the mixture into a piping bag fitted with a large star tube (tip) and pipe 18 meringues on the baking sheets. Dry out the meringues in the oven at 110°C/225°F/gas ¼ for 3-4 hours, until crisp and dry but not coloured.

Mix the strawberries with the orange liqueur in a serving bowl. Place the whipped cream in another bowl and pile the meringues in a third bowl. Let everyone help themselves to orange meringues, strawberries and cream.

ORANGE RICE PUDDING

Serves 4

Place 45 g/1½ oz/ ¼ cup pudding rice in an ovenproof dish. Add 2 tablespoons granulated sugar, 1 teaspoon natural vanilla essence (extract), the pared rind of 1 orange, 1 cinnamon stick and a little grated nutmeg. Pour in 600 ml/ 1 pint/2½ cups milk and stir well. Add a lump of butter and bake at 160°C/325°F/gas 3 for about 2½ hours, or until the pudding is creamy. Stir the pudding occasionally during the first part of cooking, then frequently for the last 30 minutes so that it becomes very creamy. Serve hot. You may like to add 60 g/2 oz/ ⅓ cup raisins about halfway through cooking.

 **Chocolate Orange Flan**

Serves 6 - 8

125 g/4 oz/ ½ cup	butter
175 g/6 oz/1½ cups	plain (all-purpose) flour
2 tablespoons	caster (superfine) sugar
About 3 tablespoons	water
125 g/4 oz/4 squares	plain (dark) chocolate, melted
	Segments from 5 oranges to decorate

Filling

30 g/1 oz/ ¼ cup	plain (all-purpose) flour
4 tablespoons	caster (superfine) sugar
3 tablespoons	cocoa
1 tablespoon	natural vanilla essence (extract)
	Grated rind and juice of 1 orange
3	egg yolks
300 ml/½ pint/1¼ cups	milk
300 ml/½ pint/1¼ cups	double (heavy) cream

Rub the butter into the flour. Stir in the sugar and mix in just enough water to bind the dough. Roll out and use to line a 23 cm/9 inch loose-bottomed flan tin (pie pan). Prick the bottom of the dough and chill for 30 minutes. Line with greaseproof (wax) paper and baking beans, and bake at 200°C/400°F/gas 6 for 15 minutes. Then remove the paper and beans, and bake for another 10 minutes. Leave to cool.

For the filling, mix the flour, caster sugar, cocoa, vanilla, grated orange rind and juice with the egg yolks until smooth, adding a little of the milk to make a smooth paste. Heat the remaining milk, pour it onto the paste and stir well. Pour the mixture back into the saucepan and bring to the boil, stirring hard all the time. Simmer for 3 minutes, then remove from the heat and cover the surface of the sauce with dampened greaseproof paper or baking parchment. Leave to cool.

Brush the melted chocolate inside the cooked flan case. Whip half the cream and fold it into the filling. Spread this over the melted chocolate and chill well. Whip the remaining cream and pipe equally spaced lines across the top of the flan. Arrange the orange segments in the gaps between the lines of cream just before serving.

 ## ORANGE SOUFFLE CREPES

SERVES 6	
6	large crêpes, see note below
30 g/1 oz/2 tablespoons	butter
30 g/1 oz/$\frac{1}{4}$ cup	plain (all-purpose) flour
	Grated rind of 1 orange and juice of 2 oranges
4 tablespoons	dry sherry
60 g/2 oz/$\frac{1}{4}$ cup	caster (superfine) sugar
2	egg whites
10	passion fruit
4 tablespoons	golden (light corn) syrup
3	oranges, segments removed

Cook the crêpes slowly so that they are very pale when set – do not allow them to brown properly or they will be overcooked in the finished dessert.

Melt the butter in a saucepan. Stir in the flour and cook for 1 minute, then add the orange rind and juice, sherry and sugar. Bring to the boil, stirring rapidly, to make a very thick sauce. Beat well to eliminate lumps and leave to cool for 15 minutes.

Grease two baking sheets. Whisk the egg whites until they are stiff but not dry. Beat about a quarter of the egg white into the orange sauce to soften it, then use a metal spoon to fold in the remaining egg white. Lay a crêpe on a baking sheet and spoon some of the soufflé mixture on one half of it, leaving a space around the edge. Fold the other half of the crêpe over. Repeat with the remaining crêpes. Bake immediately at 190°C/375°F/gas 5 for 20 minutes, or until the soufflé mixture is lightly browned.

Meanwhile, halve the passion fruit and scoop out the flesh into a sieve (strainer) placed over a small saucepan. Add the syrup and heat gently, stirring all the time. As soon as the crêpes are ready, transfer them to a warmed plate and trickle some sauce over. Decorate with orange segments and serve.

NOTE: *To make the batter, place 125g/4 oz/1 cup plain (all-purpose) flour in a bowl. Make a well in the middle and add 2 eggs. Beat in 300ml/$\frac{1}{2}$ pint/1$\frac{1}{4}$ cups milk gradually to form a smooth batter. Then beat in 1 tablespoon oil and 1 tablespoon water.*

OPPOSITE: Orange Soufflé Crêpes

 **BAKING**

The pronounced taste of orange enhances a variety of baked goods, from homely Teabread and oaty Flapjacks to interesting Citrus Sweet Potato Flan and irresistible Orange Doughnuts.

TEABREAD

MAKES a 900 g/2 lb loaf

150 g/5 oz/1 cup	raisins
150 g/5 oz/1 cup	currants
	Grated rind and juice of 1 orange
About 200 ml/7 fl oz/^{3}⁄4 cup	freshly brewed tea
250 g/9 oz/2^1⁄4 cups	self-raising (self-rising) flour
125 g/4 oz/^{3}⁄4 cup	soft brown sugar
4 tablespoons	chopped mixed peel
125 g/4 oz/1 cup	walnuts, chopped
1	egg, beaten

Mix the raisins, currants and orange rind in a bowl. Make the orange juice up to 250 ml/8 fl oz/1 cup with hot fresh tea, then pour this over the fruit and cover the bowl. Leave to stand overnight.

Base-line and grease a 900 g/2 lb loaf tin. Mix the flour, sugar, peel and walnuts in a bowl. Make a well in the middle and add the soaked fruit with all the juices scraped from the bowl. Add the egg, then mix all the ingredients thoroughly and turn the mixture into the prepared tin. Spread the mixture evenly, then bake at 160°C/325°F/gas 3 for 1^1⁄2 - 1^3⁄4 hours or until the teabread is firm, risen and browned. Turn out to cool on a wire rack. The teabread is best when allowed to mature for 1-2 days before eating. Serve sliced and buttered.

 **CITRUS SWEET POTATO FLAN**

This unusual flan is creamy and delicious – keep your friends guessing as to the identity of the main ingredient!

SERVES 8

125 g/4 oz/ ¹₂ cup	butter
60 g/2 oz/ ¹₄ cup	white vegetable fat (shortening)
225 g/8 oz/2 cups	plain (all-purpose) flour
60 g/2 oz/ ¹₄ cup	caster (superfine) sugar
125 g/4 oz/1 cup	chopped toasted hazelnuts
2-3 tablespoons	water
	Soured cream to serve

FILLING

350 g/12 oz/2 cups	sweet potatoes, boiled until tender and puréed until smooth
	Grated rind and juice of 1 orange
2 teaspoons	ground allspice
125 g/4 oz/ ¹₂ cup	caster (superfine) sugar
3	eggs, beaten
150 ml/ ¹₄ pint/ ²₃ cup	double (heavy) cream
2 tablespoons	flaked almonds
	Icing (confectioners') sugar to decorate

Rub both fats into the flour, then stir in the sugar and nuts. Mix in enough water to bind the ingredients, then roll out the dough and use to line a 25 cm/10 inch loose-bottomed flan tin (pie pan). Prick the bottom of the dough and chill for 30 minutes. Line with greaseproof (wax) paper and baking beans and bake at 200°C/400°F/gas 6 for 20 minutes. Remove the paper and beans. Reduce the oven temperature to 180°C/350°F/gas 4.

Mix the sweet potato purée, orange rind and juice, allspice, sugar, eggs and cream. Beat well, then turn the mixture into the flan case and sprinkle with the almonds. Bake for 45-50 minutes, or until the filling is set and evenly browned on top. Leave to cool. Dust with icing sugar and serve warm with soured cream.

 ## Marble Ring

MAKES a 23 cm/9 inch ring cake	125 g/4 oz/ ^{1}⁄2 cup	butter or margarine
	125 g/4 oz/ ^{1}⁄2 cup	caster (superfine) sugar
		Grated rind of 2 oranges
	2	eggs
	175 g/6 oz/1 ^{1}⁄2 cups	self-raising (self-rising) flour
		Juice of 1 orange
	2 tablespoons	cocoa
	225 g/8 oz/8 squares	plain (dark) chocolate, melted
	1 teaspoon	sweet almond oil
	125 g/4 oz/4 squares	white chocolate, melted
	1 tablespoon	icing (confectioners') sugar
	125 g/4 oz/1 cup	cream cheese
		Pared orange rind, boiled and cut into long shreds

Thoroughly grease a 23 cm/9 inch round ring tin. Cream the butter or margarine with the caster sugar and grated orange rind until very soft and creamy. Beat in the eggs, adding a little of the flour, then fold in the remaining flour. Gently stir in the orange juice. Drop spoonfuls of the mixture well apart into the tin, using only half the mixture.

Stir the cocoa into the remaining mixture, and drop spoonfuls into the tin between the plain orange mixture. Use a skewer to drag both mixtures lightly through each other. Do not overmix or the mixtures will melt together during baking. Bake at 160°C/325°F/gas 3 for 45-50 minutes, until the cake is risen, springy to the touch and slightly shrunk away from the sides of the tin. Turn out to cool on a wire rack.

Mix the melted plain chocolate with the almond oil and use this to coat the cake completely. Leave in a cool place until set – the oil will prevent the chocolate from setting hard. Beat the white chocolate and icing sugar into the cream cheese, then pipe swirls of this around the top of the cake. Decorate with shreds of orange rind.

OPPOSITE: Marble Ring

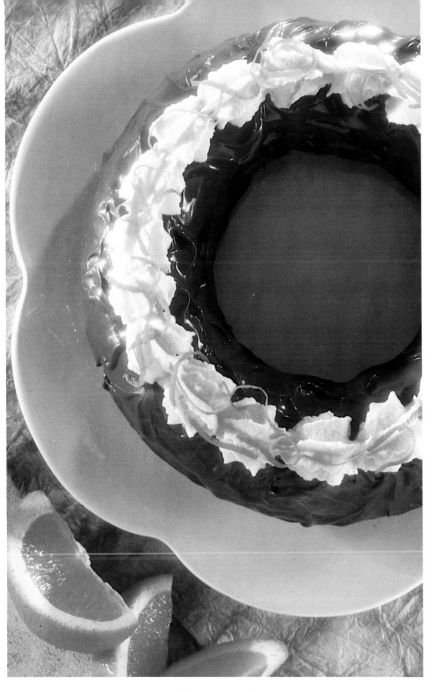

 **ORANGE SWIRLS**

MAKES 12 pairs or 24 single biscuits

275 g/10 oz/1¼ cups	unsalted butter, softened
175 g/6 oz/1 cup	icing (confectioners') sugar
	Grated rind of 2 large oranges
1 tablespoon	natural vanilla essence (extract)
175 g/6 oz/1½ cups	plain (all-purpose) flour
90 g/3 oz/¾ cup	cornflour (cornstarch)
	Juice of ½ orange
	Icing (confectioners') sugar to decorate

Grease two baking sheets. Beat 225 g/8 oz/1 cup of the butter with half the icing sugar until very soft. Beat in the rind of 1 orange and the vanilla essence, then gradually beat in the flour and cornflour. Spoon the mixture into a piping bag fitted with a large star tube (tip) and pipe 12 swirls of mixture slightly apart on each baking sheet. Chill for at least 1 hour.

Bake the biscuits at 190°C/375°F/gas 5 for 15-20 minutes, until golden. Leave to cool for a few minutes on the baking sheets, then transfer to a wire rack and leave to cool completely. Beat the remaining butter, icing sugar and orange rind, then mix in the orange juice. Sandwich the cold biscuits together with this buttercream and dust with icing sugar.

VARIATIONS

ORANGE FINGERS　Pipe the mixture in fingers. These may be part-dipped in melted plain (dark) chocolate when cold.

ORANGE PETITS FOURS Pipe small stars of the mixture and top each with a piece of candied orange peel. Bake for about 8 minutes. Drizzle melted plain (dark) chocolate over the petits fours and place them in paper sweet cases (candy cups) for serving.

 **SPECIAL FLAPJACKS**

MAKES 16 squares

These are a quick-to-make treat for tea and this spiced-up version is really delicious.

Melt 175 g/6 oz/ ^{3}⁄$_4$ cup butter or margarine with 60 g/2 oz/ ^{1}⁄$_3$ cup granulated sugar, 90 g/3 oz/3 tablespoons clear or thick honey, the grated rind and juice of 1 orange and 1 tablespoon ground cinnamon. Mix in 125 g/4 oz/1 cup chopped pecan nuts, 60 g/2 oz/ ^{1}⁄$_3$ cup sultanas (golden raisins) and 275 g/10 oz/3^1⁄$_2$ cups rolled oats. Press the mixture into a thoroughly greased 20 cm/8 inch square tin and bake at 200°C/400°F/gas 6 for about 20 minutes, until golden brown and firm on top. Cool in the tin: cut into squares while still warm and remove when completely cold.

ABOVE: Orange Swirls and fingers

 **SPECIAL-OCCASION COOKIES**

MAKES about 20

	Grated rind and juice of 1 orange
3 tablespoons	clear honey
1 teaspoon	ground cinnamon
90 g/3 oz/6 tablespoons	butter
175 g/6 oz/1½ cups	plain (all-purpose) flour

DECORATION

	Grated rind of 1 orange
225 g/8 oz/8 squares	white chocolate, melted
	Pieces of glacé (candied) fruit
	Coloured sugar strands (sprinkles)
	Silver dragees

Heat the orange rind and juice with the honey and cinnamon, stirring, until thoroughly combined. Remove the pan from the heat and stir in the butter. When the butter has melted, stir in the flour and gather the dough into a ball. Leave to cool, then chill for 30 minutes.

Grease two baking sheets. Divide the dough and roll out each half quite thinly – to about 3 mm/ ⅛ inch thickness. Stamp out the cookies using shaped cutters. Hearts, circles, diamonds, flowers and squares are all suitable shapes, while star and Christmas tree cutters can be used for Christmas. Transfer the cookies to the baking sheets. If you want to hang the cookies on a Christmas tree, remember to make a hole near the top of each one. Prick the cookies and chill them for 30 minutes before baking. Bake at 190°C/375°F/gas 5 for 15 minutes, then cool on a wire rack.

Mix the orange rind into the melted chocolate. Coat the cooled cookies with the chocolate mixture and decorate with pieces of glacé fruit, coloured strands or silver dragees just before the chocolate sets. Thread pieces of ribbon through the holes if you want to hang the cookies on a Christmas tree – they should be individually wrapped in cling film (plastic wrap) if they are left on the tree for more than a few hours.

 ## Orange Doughnuts

MAKES 20

350 g/12 oz/3 cups	strong plain (hard wheat) flour
1 teaspoon	salt
2 tablespoons	caster (superfine) sugar
	Grated rind and juice of 1 orange
3 teaspoons	fast-action yeast
60 g/2 oz/$\frac{1}{4}$ cup	butter, melted
About 6 tablespoons	orange marmalade
	Oil for deep frying
	Caster (superfine) sugar for coating

Thoroughly flour two baking sheets. Mix the flour, salt, caster sugar, orange rind and yeast in a bowl. Make the orange juice up to 250 ml/8 fl oz/1 cup with hot water, then add it to the dry ingredients with the butter. Mix well to bind the ingredients into a soft dough. Knead the dough well on a floured surface until it is smooth and elastic – this takes about 10 minutes. Roll the dough into a sausage shape and cut it into 20 equal portions. Keep the dough covered when you are not working with it.

Flatten a portion of dough on the palm of your hand and place a little marmalade in the centre. Then fold the dough around the marmalade to enclose it completely. Pinch the dough to seal in the filling thoroughly, pat it into shape and place on the baking sheet. When all the doughnuts are shaped, cover them loosely with oiled polythene and leave in a warm place until doubled in size.

Heat the oil for deep frying to 150-160°C/325-350°F. If the oil is too hot the doughnuts will brown too much. Fry the doughnuts a few at a time, turning them once or twice, until they are puffed and golden all over. Drain well on paper towels, roll them in caster sugar immediately and place on a wire rack to cool. Serve warm or cold, when they may be slit and filled with piped whipped cream.

 **SWEET NOTHINGS**

Here are a few ideas for extras – interesting concoctions with small roles to play – and confectionery. They all make splendid gifts and they are fun to prepare.

ORANGE BUTTER

Beat the grated rind of 1 orange, 4 tablespoons icing (confectioners') sugar and 1-2 tablespoons brandy into 125 g/ 4 oz/ $\frac{1}{2}$ cup unsalted butter. Serve with waffles, pancakes, hot toasted English muffins or grilled (broiled) bananas.

ORANGE PEEL IN BRANDY

Scrape the thick pith from the back of orange peel, then cut the peel into thick strips. Cook the strips of peel in steadily simmering water for about 20 minutes, or until tender. Reserve 125 ml/4 fl oz/ $\frac{1}{2}$ cup of the cooking water and use to make a syrup with 225 g/8 oz/1 cup granulated sugar. Boil, then remove from the heat and add an equal volume of brandy. Pack the peel loosely into jars and cover with the brandy syrup. Cover with airtight lids. Allow to mature for a week before using. Chop the peel for use on desserts or in baking. Use it as a decoration or topping for ice-cream. Spoon the syrup over waffles, profiteroles or fruit salad.

ORANGES IN BRANDY

Peel and thickly slice the fruit. Prepare the syrup as in previous recipe, with an equal volume of brandy. Pack the orange slices loosely into a wide-necked jar, adding a cinnamon stick if liked, then cover completely with the brandy syrup. Cover and chill for 2 days before using. Use within 2-3 weeks.

 ## ORANGE DELIGHT

This is a variation on the Turkish delight theme.

MAKES about 900 g/2 lb

	Grated rind and juice of 2 oranges
	Juice of 2 lemons
675 g/1¹₂ lb/3 cups	granulated sugar
1 tablespoon	natural vanilla essence (extract)
400 ml/14 fl oz/1³₄ cups	water
4 tablespoons	gelatine
2 tablespoons	cornflour (cornstarch)
125 g/4 oz/²₃ cup	icing (confectioners') sugar

Place the orange rind and juice, lemon juice, sugar and vanilla in a saucepan. Pour 6 tablespoons of the water into a heatproof bowl and sprinkle the gelatine over it, then set aside. Add the remaining water to the sugar mixture.

Heat the mixture, stirring until the sugar has dissolved, then bring to the boil and stop stirring. Boil until the syrup reaches the soft ball stage: 115°C/235°F on a sugar thermometer or until a little of the mixture forms a soft ball when dropped into cold water and kneaded between the fingertips.

Stand the bowl of gelatine over the saucepan and stir until the gelatine has dissolved completely. Add a ladleful of the syrup to the gelatine, stir well, then pour it back into the main batch of syrup. Rinse a 15 cm/6 in square tin with cold water and pour in the mixture. Leave to cool, then chill.

Mix the cornflour and icing sugar. Use a knife dipped in cornflour to cut the orange delight into chunks, then roll each one in the sugar and cornflour mixture.

NEXT PAGE: LEFT TO RIGHT: Orange Delight; Stuffed Fresh Dates (p.62); Oranges in Brandy; Orange Peel in Brandy

 ## STUFFED FRESH DATES

Arrange these on an attractive platter with the
Orange Delight to serve with coffee after dinner
instead of the usual mints.

MAKES 12

	Grated rind and juice of 1 orange
60 g/2 oz/ ¼ cup	*granulated sugar*
125 g/4 oz/1¼ cups	*ground almonds*
2 tablespoons	*chopped pistachio nuts*
12	*fresh dates, pitted, skinned and split open*
	Caster (superfine) sugar for coating
	Halved pistachio nuts to decorate

Place the orange rind and juice in a small saucepan with the sugar and heat gently, stirring all the time, until the sugar
has dissolved. Bring to the boil and boil hard for 2 minutes, then remove from the heat. Mix in the ground almonds
and pistachio nuts to make a thick paste. Allow to cool.

Roll a small portion of the paste into a sausage shape and press into a split date. When all the dates are filled, roll
them in caster sugar and arrange them in paper sweet cases (candy cups). Decorate with halved pistachio nuts.

INDEX

Arabian Orange Salad 15
Avocados, baked 16

Barley with orange pesto 36
Beetroot and orange chutney 37
Brandy, orange peel in 58
Brandy, oranges in 58
Buck's fizz 10

Caramelized orange profiteroles 43
Carrot salad, zesty 18
Chocolate orange flan 47
Chocolates, speedy orange 8
Citrus sweet potato flan 51
Cookies, special-occasion 56
Crêpes, orange soufflé 48
Crystallized peel, one-step 9

Dates, stuffed fresh 62
Doughnuts, orange 57
Duck bigarrade 25

Emmenthal tart 29
Exotic bath bouquet 14

Fettucini with bacon and fennel 31
Flapjacks, special 55

Garnishes and decorations 8

Ice-cream, rich orange 42

Lamb, orange-glazed 25

Marble ring 52
Marzipan oranges 8
Mushrooms, orange marinated 17
Mussels with garlic-orange sauce 20
Mustard orange dressing 18

One-pot sauté 34
Orange butter 58
Orange delight 59
Orange night-light 14
Orange and peach preserve, rich 39
Orange redcurrent jelly 40
Orange soufflé crêpes 48
Orange swirls 54
Orange tea 10
Oranges:
    buying, storing, preparing 7
    types of 6

Peel rope 12
Pesto, orange (with barley) 36

Pickled onions, special 41
Piquant rarebit 19
Pork, skewered 26
Pot-pourri, lasting 12
    orange and herb 12
Profiteroles, caramelized orange 43

Red cabbage, refreshing 18
Redcurrant jelly, orange 40
Rice pudding, orange 46
Rum cooler, orange 10

Salad, new potato salad with salami 35
Seville refresher 10
Sizzling steak 28
Strawberries with orange meringues 46

Teabread 50
Tomato chutney, zesty 38
Tomato and orange salad 18
Tuna with orange 21
Turkey olives 24

Veal and ham loaf 30

Vodka or brandy, orange 10